MLB's Greatest Teams

MINNESOTA TWINS

Caroline Wesley

Big Buddy Books
An Imprint of Abdo Publishing
abdobooks.com

abdobooks.com

Published by Abdo Publishing, a division of ABDO, PO Box 398166, Minneapolis, Minnesota 55439.

Printed in the United States of America, North Mankato, Minnesota.
102018
012019

THIS BOOK CONTAINS RECYCLED MATERIALS

Cover Photo: Duane Burleson/Getty Images.
Interior Photos: 33ft/Depositphotos (p. 7); Al Bello/Getty Images (p. 21); AP Images (p. 23); Brian Blanco/Getty Images (pp. 24, 25); Brian Toovalian/AP Images (p. 13); David Durochik/AP Images (p. 22); Duane Burleson/AP Images (p. 15); Gene Herrick/AP Images (p. 11); Hannah Foslien/Getty Images (pp. 5, 9, 17); Harold Valentine/AP Images (p. 22); Jason Miller/Getty Images (p. 27); Jason Wachter/AP Images (p. 28); Jim Mone/AP Images (p. 29); Ronald Martinez/Getty Images (p. 19).

Coordinating Series Editor: Tamara L. Britton
Contributing Series Editor: Jill M. Roesler
Graphic Design: Jenny Christensen, Cody Laberda

Library of Congress Control Number: 2018948449

Publisher's Cataloging-in-Publication Data

Names: Wesley, Caroline, author.
Title: Minnesota Twins / by Caroline Wesley.
Description: Minneapolis, Minnesota : Abdo Publishing, 2019 | Series: MLB's greatest teams set 2 | Includes online resources and index.
Identifiers: ISBN 9781532118104 (lib. bdg.) | ISBN 9781532171147 (ebook)
Subjects: LCSH: Minnesota Twins (Baseball team)--Juvenile literature. | Baseball teams--United States--History--Juvenile literature. | Major League Baseball (Organization)--Juvenile literature. | Baseball--Juvenile literature.
Classification: DDC 796.35764--dc23

Contents

Major League Baseball

The Minnesota Twins is one of 30 Major League Baseball (MLB) teams. The team plays in the American League Central **Division**.

Throughout the season, all MLB teams play 162 games. The season begins in April and can continue until November.

League Play

There are two leagues in MLB. They are the American League (AL) and the National League (NL). Each league has 15 teams and is split into three divisions. They are east, central, and west.

TC Bear joined the team as the Twins' mascot in 2000. He likes to appear at hospitals, schools, and parades to meet his fans.

A Winning Team

The Twins team is from Minneapolis and St. Paul, Minnesota. The team's colors are navy, scarlet, gold, and white.

The team has had good seasons and bad. But time and again, the players have proven themselves. Let's see what makes the Twins one of MLB's greatest teams!

Fast Facts

HOME FIELD: Target Field

TEAM COLORS: Navy, scarlet, gold, and white

TEAM SONG: "We're Gonna Win, Twins!" by Ray Charles and Dick Wilson

PENNANTS: 6

WORLD SERIES TITLES: 1924, 1987, 1991

CANADA
UNITED STATES OF AMERICA
MEXICO
CANADA
North Dakota
Minnesota
LAKE SUPERIOR
South Dakota
Minneapolis
St. Paul
Wisconsin
Iowa
N
W
E
S

Target Field

Before the team became the Twins, it was called the Washington Senators. The team played in two different parks in Washington, DC.

In 1961, the ball team moved to Minnesota and became the Twins. Players first competed at the Metropolitan Stadium. They moved to the Metrodome in 1982.

Finally in 2010, the Twins moved to its current home at Target Field. The team beat the Boston Red Sox in its first game in the new stadium.

A large sign in centerfield shows the Twins characters Minnie and Paul. The sign lights up when a Twins player hits a home run!

Then and Now

The Twins team was named for the twin cities Minneapolis and St. Paul. In its fifth year as the Twins, the team made it to the World Series. But the players could not defeat Los Angeles Dodgers' pitcher Sandy Koufax.

The Twins made it to the **playoffs** again in 1969 and 1970. Both years, the team won AL **division** titles.

Minnesota's public leaders welcomed the state's new baseball team in November 1960.

The team placed in the lower half of its **division** many times during the early 1980s. In 1986, players placed sixth out of seven teams in the AL West.

The next year, the Twins climbed all the way up to the **playoffs**. There, the team collected its fifth AL **pennant**. And players won their first World Series title as the Twins!

In 1991, the team earned its second World Series title. But the Twins struggled on the field during the rest of the 1990s. Finally in 2001, the team made a comeback.

The Twins was the first team featured on a Wheaties cereal box. It was an image of the team after winning the 1987 World Series!

Highlights

After an eight-year losing streak, the Twins' luck began to change. From 2002 to 2006, the team took home four AL Central **Division** titles!

Three years later, the Twins and the Detroit Tigers were tied for the Central Division title. The two teams faced off in a single game. Twelve exciting **innings** later, the Twins beat the Tigers. And the Minnesota team went into another **playoff** season.

More than 3.2 million fans attended Twins baseball games in 2010.

The Twins won the AL Central **Division** title in 2009 and 2010. But players did not make it past the AL Division Series either year.

After two **playoff** appearances, the Twins suffered six losing seasons from 2011 to 2016. Then in 2017, the team went to the playoffs as a **wild-card** team. It was the first team to go into **postseason** having lost more than 100 games the year before!

Win or Go Home

The top team from each AL and NL division goes to the playoffs. Each league also sends one wild-card team. One team from the AL and one from the NL will win the pennant. The two pennant winners then go to the World Series!

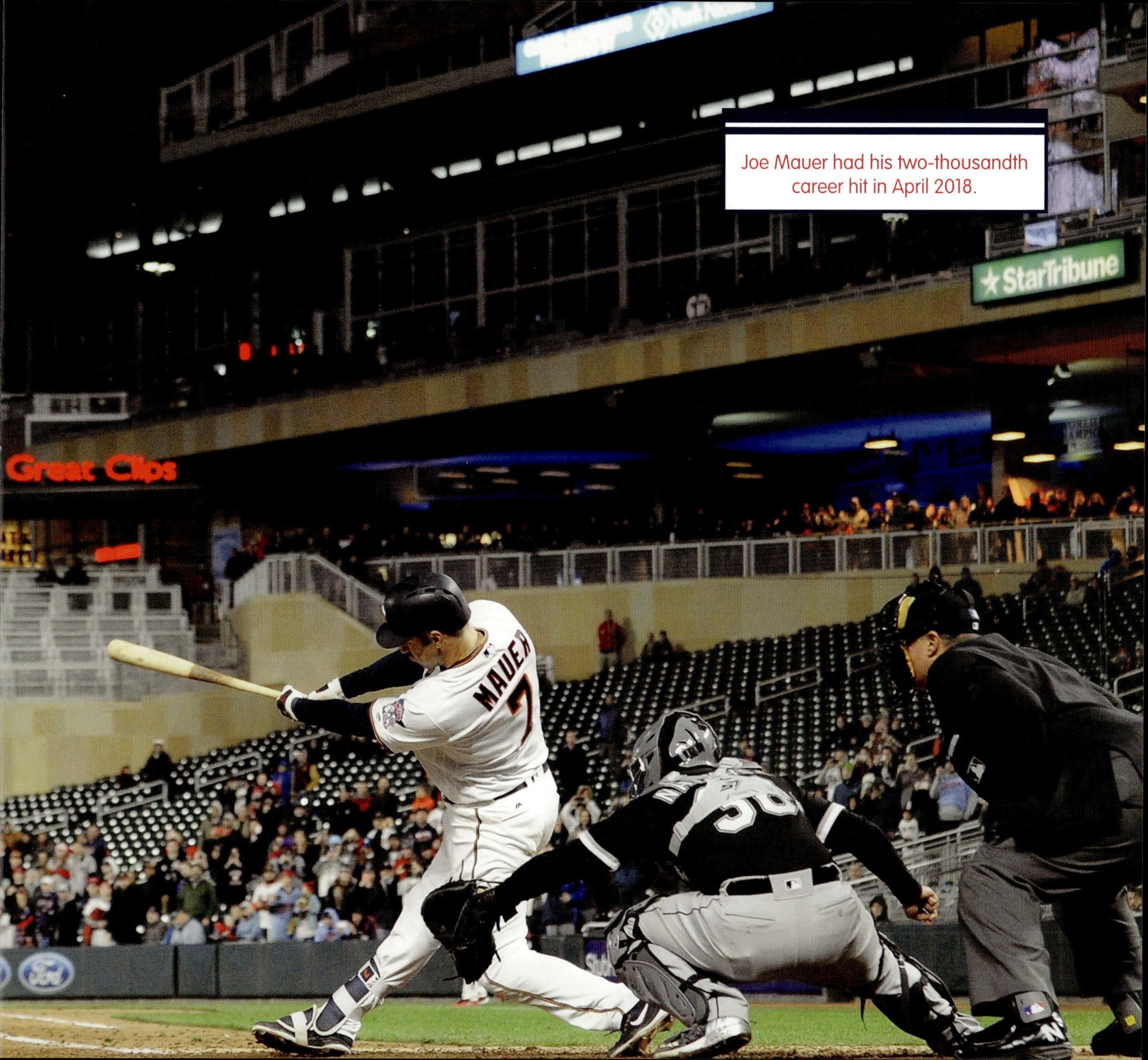

Joe Mauer had his two-thousandth career hit in April 2018.

Famous Managers

Manager Tom Kelly joined the Twins in 1986. He managed the team his entire **career**.

During his first full year, Kelly led the Twins to the 1987 World Series title. And he helped them to another World Series victory four years later. For this, Kelly won the 1991 AL Manager of the Year Award.

In 16 years with the Twins, Kelly led the team to 1,140 wins. The Twins **retired** Kelly's jersey number 10 in 2012.

In 2017, the Twins put up a monument at Target Field to honor Tom Kelly.

Paul Molitor was a **designated hitter** and first baseman for the Twins from 1996 to 1998. He began managing the team in 2015. In his third year, he helped the team back from a losing 2016 season. He led the Twins to 85 wins in 2017.

That year, his managing helped the team make its first **playoff** appearance since 2010. Molitor earned the 2017 AL Manager of the Year Award for his leadership.

As a player, Molitor earned a spot in the National Baseball Hall of Fame.

Star Players

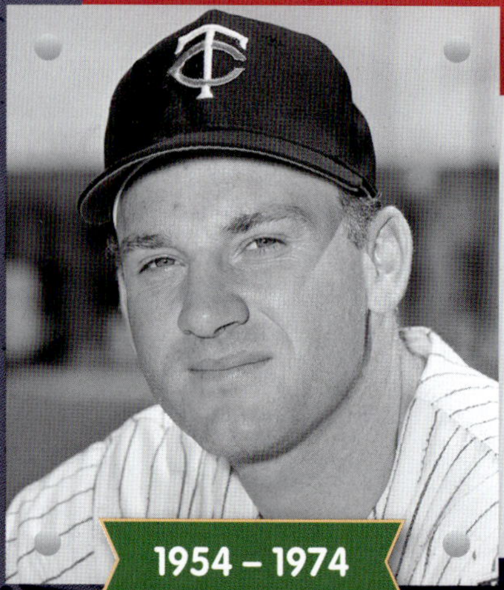

1954 – 1974

Harmon Killebrew FIRST AND THIRD BASEMAN, #3

Harmon Killebrew was the most skilled batter of his time. Nicknamed "the Killer" at bat, he hit 559 home runs with the Twins. And he had more than 1,500 **runs batted in (RBIs)**. Killebrew played all but one game in the 1969 regular season. That year, he earned the 1969 AL **Most Valuable Player (MVP)** Award.

Tony Oliva RIGHTFIELDER, #6

A Cuban native, Tony Oliva came to the US in 1960. Beginning in 1962, he played for the Twins his entire **career**. After scoring 109 runs and 32 home runs, he earned **Rookie** of the Year in 1964. Oliva led the league in hits five times from 1964 to 1970. For his outfielding, Oliva also earned a **Gold Glove** in 1966.

1962 – 1976

Rod Carew FIRST AND SECOND BASEMAN, #29

During his Twins **career**, Rod Carew **putout** more than 2,500 runners on second base. And he putout more than 4,300 on first base! But Carew was best at batting. He earned seven batting titles and scored 950 runs with the Twins. In 1977, he earned both the AL **MVP** and the Major League Player of the Year awards.

Kirby Puckett CENTERFIELDER, #34

Kirby Puckett spent his entire career with the Twins. As a batter, he scored more than 1,000 runs for the team. He earned six **Silver Sluggers** for his batting. As an outfielder, Puckett putout more than 4,400 batters. He won six **Gold Gloves** for his fielding skills. Puckett joined the National Baseball Hall of Fame in 2001.

Brian Dozier SECOND BASEMAN, #2

Brian Dozier joined the team in 2012. In 2015, he hit 28 home runs. This earned him a spot on the AL All-Star team. His skills improved the following year with 42 home runs and 99 **RBIs**. Dozier was the top Twins player in 2014 and 2016. And in 2017, he won his first Gold Glove for his talent on the field.

Joe Mauer CATCHER AND FIRST BASEMAN, #7

In 2006, Joe Mauer became the first AL catcher to win a batting title. He also earned his first **Silver Slugger**. Since then, he has earned two more batting titles and four more Sluggers. Mauer has also earned three **Gold Gloves** for his talent as catcher. In 2009, he took home the AL **MVP** Award.

Byron Buxton CENTERFIELDER, #25

The Twins **drafted** Byron Buxton in 2012 in the first round. Five years later, Buxton began to see great success. In 2017, he earned the **Gold Glove** and **Platinum Glove** awards as centerfielder. In only four seasons with the Twins, he **putout** nearly 800 batters! For this, he earned the 2017 Wilson Overall Defensive Player Award.

Miguel Sanó THIRD BASEMAN, #22

Miguel Sanó impressed his team from the start. In his first year, he hit 18 home runs as **designated hitter**! For this, he earned the **Rookie** of the Month Award for August 2015. As a third baseman, he putout more than 120 batters in only four seasons.

Final Call

The Twins have a long, rich history. The team has played in six World Series, and earned three World Series titles.

Even during losing seasons, true fans have stuck by the players. Many believe the Twins will remain one of the greatest teams in MLB.

All-Stars

The best players from both leagues come together each year for the All-Star Game. This game does not count toward the regular season records. It is simply to celebrate the best players in MLB.

Leftfielder Eddie Rosario hit more than 20 home runs in 2018. He hit three of those homers in a single game!

Through the Years

1924

The Washington Senators won the World Series.

1955

The 1955 Harmon Killebrew baseball card sold for $15,600 in April 2018.

1965

Players held onto a first-place lead throughout the 1965 season. The team finished the season with its first AL **pennant** as the Twins!

1985

The Twins hosted its first All-Star Game at the Metrodome.

1991

Game Six of the World Series went into overtime. In the eleventh **inning**, Kirby Puckett hit a home run! The team went on to Game Seven. There, they won their second World Series as the Twins!

1999

The Twins had 17 **rookie** players on its **roster**.

2010

The team played its first game at Target Field on April 12, 2010. Eight months later, the roof of the Metrodome caved in because of heavy snow.

2018

On April 7, the team played in the coldest game in Twins history. It was only 27°F (-3°C)!

Glossary

career a period of time spent in a certain job.

designated hitter a player who is chosen at the beginning of a game to bat in place of the pitcher and who does not play a position in the field.

division a number of teams grouped together in a sport for competitive purposes.

draft a system for professional sports teams to choose new players.

Gold Glove Award annually given to the MLB players with the best fielding experience.

inning a division of a baseball game that consists of a turn at bat for each team.

Most Valuable Player (MVP) the player who contributes the most to his or her team's success.

pennant the prize that is awarded to the champions of the two MLB leagues each year.

Platinum Glove Award fans vote for the season's best defensive player who has also won a Gold Glove Award.

playoffs a game or series of games to determine a championship or to break a tie.

postseason a period of time immediately after the regular season. Teams will play against each other in a series of games to find a winner.

putout an action that causes a batter or runner on the opposite team to be out.

retire to withdraw from use or service.

rookie a player who is new to the major leagues until he meets certain criteria.

roster an orderly list of people belonging to a professional sports group.

run batted in (RBI) a run that is scored as a result of a batter's hit, walk, or stolen base.

Silver Slugger Award given every year to the best offensive players in MLB.

wild-card a player or team chosen to fill a place in a competition after the regularly qualified players or teams have all been decided.

Index